G000111629

dudley

acknowledgements

I'd like to thank Alison John for keeping me
and all the recipes in order; Aled Llŷr for his
support and friendship; the lads who have been
with me since the start – Gerry Wakeham and
Peter Moscrop – and, occasionally, Peter
Dunbar Collis – if he's not shopping! Thanks to
Chris Winter for his superb music and John
'Chwc' Gillanders for his editing and fantastic
dedication. Without their support this book
would not be in the shops today.
Thanks to you all.

dudley

yl Lolfa

'Wales: the True Taste' is the brand for the food and drink industry in Wales. It is a promise that Welsh food and drink is pure, natural, and appetising; produced with integrity and care. **Wales: the True Taste** is managed by the Welsh Development Agency, for more information contact **www.walesthetruetaste.com** or **telephone 08457 775577**

First impression: 2003

Design: Ceri Jones
Food Photographer: Simon Regan
Food Stylist: Beverly Reed
Dudley Photographs: Huw John

ISBN: 0 86243 695 8

Published and printed in Wales
by Y Lolfa Cyf., Talybont, Ceredigion SY24 5AP
e-mail ylolfa@ylolfa.com
website www.ylolfa.com
tel (01970) 832 304
fax 832 782
isdn 832 813

Contents

Soup

Fish

Sauces, Stuffing and Relish

Meat

Chicken

Pasta and Rice

Vegetables

Vegetarian

Desserts

foreword

When we began the the first series of *Dudley* ten years ago, things were rather different. We had to make sure that the majority of the ingredients were bought in Cardiff, as many of them were impossible to find outside the capital city. Recipes were adapted and tailored to bear this in mind.

Keeping things simple was the message, and that's what I did with my first book, published in 1996. I still believe that simplicity is the key to good cooking. In this book I have made the recipes easy to follow, featuring ingredients that are now widely available.

Don't forget – buying fresh, local produce in season is a great start to any meal.

All that's left for you to do now is to get stuck in and enjoy yourself!

Dudley

soup

scotch broth

Serves 6
700g/1½ lbs of beef, cubed
2.25 litres/4 pints of water
200g/7 oz of carrots – finely chopped
200g/7 oz of turnip – finely chopped
150g/5 oz of dried marrowfat peas – soaked overnight, drained and rinsed
75g/3 oz of pearl barley – soaked overnight and drained
25g/1 oz of parsley (including the stalks)
1 tablespoons of olive oil
1 onion – finely chopped
sea salt and black pepper

Method
Fry the beef in the oil until browned.

Add the onion, salt and pepper.

While the meat is cooking, simmer the water in a large saucepan.
Add the carrots, the peas, the pearl barley, the turnip, the browned
meat and half the parsley, and cook for 1 hour on a low heat.

Bring to the boil and simmer for a further half an hour, or until the
meat is tender.

Add the remaining parsley, and season to taste.

mint and pea soup

Serves 4

900g/2 lbs of fresh peas
1.1 litres/2 pints of vegetable or chicken stock
225ml/8 fl oz of single cream
1 bunch of fresh mint – chopped
1 onion – finely chopped
2 tablespoons of olive oil
1 teaspoon of lemon juice (optional)
sea salt and black pepper

Method

Heat the oil in a sufficiently large saucepan. Cook the onion until soft under a lid to sweat and avoid colouring.

Add the stock and bring to the boil before adding the peas, salt and pepper. Boil for 2–3 minutes.

Add the mint and the cream and adjust for seasoning again (add the lemon juice if using).

Leave to cool for a while before liquidizing until smooth.

To serve – the soup can be eaten hot or cold with a drop of cream or crème fraîche.

thai chicken and noodle soup

Serves 2

2 chicken breasts – cut into strips

570ml/1 pint of chicken stock

3–4 mushrooms – quartered

3 cloves of garlic – sliced

2 small red chillies (hot)

2 tablespoons of sesame oil

1 tablespoon of Thai fish sauce (nam pla) or light soy sauce

2.5cm/1" piece of fresh ginger – thinly sliced

juice of 1 lime

fresh noodles or 1 packet of dried thai rice noodles

2 Chinese leaves

To serve

2 spring onions – finely chopped

handful of fresh coriander – finely chopped

bunch of raw beansprouts

few drops of hot chilli and garlic sauce

Method

In a large saucepan or wok, heat the oil and fry the chicken. Add the ginger and the garlic and cook lightly.

Add the mushrooms, stock, the chillies, the lime juice and the nam pla. Mix thoroughly before adding the noodles.

Simmer for 4 minutes until the noodles are cooked.

Place the Chinese leaves in the bottom of a serving dish and pour the hot soup over them.

To serve – garnish with the spring onions, the coriander, the beansprouts and the hot chilli sauce.

potato and chive soup

Serves 4–6
450g/1 lb of potatoes – thinly sliced (not cooked)
1.1 litres/2 pints of vegetable or chicken stock
150ml/2 fl oz of single cream
25g/1 oz of Welsh butter
1 onion – thinly sliced
1 leek – the white part sliced
handful of fresh parsley – finely chopped
handful of fresh chives – finely chopped
sea salt and black pepper

To serve
packet of real crisps
grated Welsh cheese

Method
Melt the butter and fry the onions in a saucepan or deep pan (using a lid so that they are not browned).

Add the stock, potatoes, bay leaf, salt and pepper and boil them until the potatoes 'melt' into the water. Leave to cool before liquidizing.

Whilst liquidizing, add the parsley and chives.

To serve – serve in a bowl topped with finely-chopped crisps, a handful of cheese and a little cream.

mushroom soup

Serves 4
450g/1 lb mushrooms – sliced
1.1 litres/2 pints vegetable stock
55ml/2 fl oz of single cream
50g/2 oz of butter
2 onions – finely chopped
2 cloves of garlic – crushed
1 sprig of tarragon
1 glass of white wine

Method

Melt the butter in a frying pan. Add the onion and the garlic and cook for a few minutes.

Add the mushrooms and fry for a further 5 minutes (place a lid over the pan to aid the cooking process and to keep the mushrooms white).

Add the wine and reduce before adding the stock. Simmer for 15 minutes.

Add the tarragon and the cream and leave to bubble for 2 minutes.

Leave to cool for a while before liquidizing it to make a smooth soup.

pumpkin soup

Serves 6
900g/2 lbs of pumpkin – peeled and deseeded and cut into large chunks
2.25 litres/4 pints of chicken or vegetable stock
50g/2 oz of butter
2 potatoes – roughly chopped
1 onion – sliced
1 carrot – roughly chopped
2.5cm/1" piece of fresh ginger – finely chopped
1 tablespoon of olive oil
sea salt and black pepper

To serve
coriander
crème fraîche

Method
Melt the butter and the oil in a frying pan.

Fry the onion, the carrot and the potatoes. Add the ginger, place a lid on the pan and allow to soften.

Add the pumpkin, fry for a while and then add the stock and seasoning to taste.

Bring to the boil and leave to bubble until the vegetables are cooked.

Leave the soup to cool before liquidizing until smooth.

To serve – serve hot in a clean pumpkin shell topped with the coriander and the crème fraîche.

fish

fillet of halibut in a cream and smoked salmon sauce

Serves 2
2 pieces of halibut
275ml/½ pint of fish stock
150ml/¼ pint of double cream
100ml/3½ fl oz of Alsace wine
75g/3 oz smoked salmon – cut into strips
1 Savoy cabbage – cut into thin strips
1 tablespoon of butter
sea salt and black pepper

Method

Fold the halibut in half and steam for about 5 minutes.

In a frying pan, boil the wine and reduce.

Add the stock, and heat before adding the cream and smoked salmon. Heat through.

In another frying pan, melt a knob of butter and lightly fry the cabbage until crisp

To serve – serve the halibut on a bed of cabbage, with a drizzle of sauce.

hot roasted salmon on a bed of warm salad

Serves 4

200g/7 oz of Glangwili smoked salmon
200g/7 oz of new potatoes – cooked and halved
4 tablespoons of walnut oil
2 tablespoons of raspberry vinegar
1 red onion – sliced
1 red pepper – roasted and skin removed
110g/4 oz of cherry tomatoes – halved
1 packet of mixed salad
1 packet of rocket
1 bunch of basil – roughly chopped
1 lemon
sea salt and black pepper

Method

Remove the skin from the salmon and break the fish into pieces. Place on one side.

Fry the onions for 1 minute.

Halve the potatoes.

Slice the pepper into strips and add to the onions.

Add the tomatoes and raspberry vinegar and heat the ingredients.

Put the rocket, salad and basil in a large mixing bowl and add the warm ingredients to them and mix well.

Add the salmon and season before serving.

To serve – lemon slices can also be added.

spicy crab filo parcels

Serves 6–8
1 spider crab, cooked (brown and white meat)
2–3 cloves of garlic – finely chopped
25g/1 oz melted butter
1 red chilli – finely chopped
1 bunch of coriander – finely chopped
1 bunch of parsley – finely chopped
1 teaspoon of cumin
1 packet of filo pastry
juice of 1 lemon
vegetable oil, to fry parcels
sea salt and black pepper

Method
In a large mixing bowl mix the crab, chilli, lemon juice, garlic, cumin, parsley and coriander. Mix well before seasoning.

Set aside to prepare the filo pastry.

Spread two layers of filo with melted butter – work quickly, as the filo dries out rapidly. 2–3 pieces of filo are required for each parcel.

Place a spoonful of the crab mixture in the centre of the filo and fold each corner to create a parcel.

Wrap the parcel in another layer of filo before deep-frying in hot oil for 4–6 minutes until lightly browned.

To serve – serve hot with a wedge of lemon.

enlli lobster

Serves 2
450–680g/1–1½ lbs of Enlli lobster
juice of half a lemon
olive oil
fresh parsley
sea salt and black pepper

To serve
salad
lemon
parsley
olive oil

Method
Boil the lobster in a large saucepan of boiling water for 15–20 minutes. Leave to cool in cold water.

Cut the lobster in half and release the meat from the tail.

Take the white meat from the claws and place all the meat back into the shell.

Place the lobster on a tray or in a frying pan. Season with sea salt, black pepper, lemon juice, parsley and a drizzle of olive oil.

Cook under a hot grill for 5–10 minutes until warmed through.

To serve – place half the lobster on a plate with salad leaves of your choice and a wedge of fresh lemon.

skate with caramelised garlic and sherry vinegar

Serves 4

The fish
4 skate wings (about 250g/9 oz each)
4 tablespoons of olive oil

The sauce
6 tablespoons of sherry vinegar
5 cloves of garlic – thinly sliced
1 tablespoon of olive oil
1 teaspoon of paprika
1 lemon – quartered

To serve
½ teaspoon of paprika
sea salt and black pepper

Method
Season the fish.

Heat the oil in a baking tray and seal the fish on both sides.

Bake in the oven at a temperature of 220°C/ Gas Mark 7 for 10–12 minutes.

The sauce – in a pan, fry the garlic in a drop of oil. Add the paprika, sherry vinegar, and salt and pepper. Reduce.

To serve – serve hot with the sauce over the fish with a light sprinkling of paprika and garnished with a piece of lemon.

mussels in a thai sauce

Serves 4
2 kg/4½ lbs of mussels – washed
200ml/7 oz of fish or chicken stock
2 lime leaves
1–2 teaspoons of nam pla
1 tablespoon of sesame oil
5cm/2" piece of lemon grass – finely chopped
2.5cm/1" piece of ginger – peeled and finely chopped
1 red chilli – sliced
1 green chilli – sliced
½ onion – finely chopped
½ tin of coconut milk
zest and juice of 1 lime
handful of coriander leaves – finely chopped

Method

In a large saucepan, heat the oil and cook the ginger, lemon grass, onions, chilli and lime leaves for approximately 2 minutes.

Add the coconut milk and simmer for a while before adding the stock, nam pla, lime juice and coriander.

Add the mussels to the ingredients. Place a lid on the saucepan and cook until the mussels have opened (approximately 2 minutes).

To serve – serve hot with a sprinkling of fresh coriander.

salmon wrapped in bacon

Serves 2
2 pieces of salmon – skinless
2 slices dry cured bacon
handful of fresh thyme
olive oil

The sauce
200g/7 oz of butter – cold
125ml/¼ pint dry white wine
125ml/¼ pint of single cream
onion, finely chopped
1 teaspoon of lemon juice
zest of 1 lemon
handful of fresh parsley – finely chopped
sea salt and black pepper

Method

Put two pieces of bacon side by side on a plate. Place one of the salmon pieces on the bacon. Sprinkle a little salt and black pepper on the salmon, add some thyme and wrap the bacon around it. Repeat with the other piece.

Brush a little olive oil over the bacon.

Cook under a warm grill or on a barbecue for around 8–10 minutes.

Remove the salmon from the grill/barbecue and set aside on a plate.

The sauce – while the salmon is cooking, heat the wine in a saucepan and leave to reduce a little.

Add the cream and bring to the boil, stirring constantly.

Cut the butter into small pieces and add to the sauce a little at a time whilst stirring constantly with a whisk.

Finally, add the lemon juice and zest, some salt and pepper and beat with the whisk. Just before serving, add parsley to the sauce.

To serve – serve with new potatoes and fresh vegetables.

salmon and orange parcels

Serves 2
2 salmon pieces
8 orange slices
bunch of fresh tarragon
splash of white wine
sea salt and black pepper

Method

Place 2 pieces of foil one on top of the other (for each parcel).

Place two pieces of orange and a few tarragon leaves on the foil.

Place the salmon on the top.

Add a little salt and black pepper over the fish before covering with some more tarragon, two further pieces of orange and a splash of wine.

Seal the parcels tightly and cook in the oven for 10–15 minutes at 160°C/Gas Mark 3.

Serve hot or cold.

wild trout and salsa

Serves 1
1 fresh brown trout
olive oil

The sauce
4 tablespoons of olive oil
2 whole cloves of garlic
pieces of lemon rind
a handful of fresh basil leaves
sea salt and black pepper

The salsa
4 tomatoes (not too soft) – roughly chopped
½ red onion – thinly sliced
a handful of green olives – sliced
a handful of fresh parsley – finely chopped
lemon juice

Method
Cover the trout with salt, black pepper and some olive oil and wrap in foil.
Place on a barbecue or under a moderate grill and cook for 8–10 minutes.

The sauce – heat the olive oil in a pan and add the lemon rind, garlic and
basil and heat through.

The salsa – put all the salsa ingredients in a bowl and mix together before
adding the lemon juice.

Then add the warm sauce, salt and black pepper and mix well.

To serve – serve with the trout.

sauces, stuffing and relish

mango stuffing

2 fresh mangoes – cubed
2 onions – roughly chopped
2–3 cloves of garlic – finely chopped
25g/1 oz of butter – for frying
1 tablespoons of dried currants
1 tablespoons of dried sultanas
1 tablespoons of dried raisins
½ loaf of bread, crumbed
bunch of fresh mint – chopped
bunch of parsley – chopped
sea salt and black pepper – to taste

Method

Melt the butter in a large frying pan. Fry the onions and garlic until soft.

Add the mint and parsley and heat through, before adding the dried fruit.
Mix well.

Add the breadcrumbs, mango, salt and pepper.

Heat through for 2–3 minutes.

Leave to cool before serving. The stuffing is suitable for chicken,
or on the side with pork.

spicy apple chutney

900g/2 lbs of eating apples – peeled, cored
   and chopped
450g/1 lb of onions – finely chopped
250ml/8¾ fl oz of cider vinegar
200g/7¼ oz of soft brown sugar
150g/5¼ oz of raisins
50g/2 oz of butter – to fry
2–3 cloves of garlic
2 teaspoons of powdered ginger
2 teaspoons of salt
1 lemon – zest and pieces
1 teaspoon of mixed spice
½ teaspoon of cayenne pepper
½ teaspoon of dried chillies

Method

Heat the butter in a large frying pan. Fry the onions and garlic until soft.

Add the ginger, mixed spice, cayenne pepper and chillies and mix well.

Add the brown sugar, vinegar, raisins and salt and stir well.

Finally, add the apple, zest and pieces of lemon to the ingredients and leave
to simmer for one hour on a low heat.

Cool before serving.

tomato and coriander relish

1 tin of chopped tomatoes
1 bunch of fresh coriander
3 cloves of garlic
juice of 2 limes
1 tablespoon of tomato ketchup
1 red onion – cubed
2.5cm/1" piece of ginger – peeled
1 teaspoon of cumin
sea salt and black pepper

Method

Place the coriander, garlic, ginger, lime juice, onion, cumin, ketchup, salt and pepper in a food processor until finely chopped.

Pour in the tomatoes and mix well before serving.

yoghurt and chilli relish

1 tub of Greek yoghurt
4 hot chillies – finely chopped
2 tablespoons of Welsh honey
bunch of fresh mint – finely chopped
sea salt and black pepper

Method

Mix all of the ingredients in a bowl, then refrigerate
for an hour before using.

Add the chillies according to your personal taste.
If you use fewer chillies, use less honey.

Both relishes are excellent accompaniments to lamb,
chicken, vegetarian burgers, cheese sandwiches –
in fact, anything that needs a bit of 'oomph'!

meat

pork in marsala sauce

Serves 2
450g/1 lb fillet of Welsh pork
425ml/15 fl oz of chicken stock
150g/5 oz of plain flour
100ml/3 fl oz of dry Marsala wine
3 tablespoons of Welsh butter
3 tablespoons of olive oil
1 fennel bulb – thinly sliced
1 red pepper
1 courgette – thickly sliced at an angle
sea salt and black pepper

Method

Escalope the pork by placing between 2 layers of cling film and flatten with a hammer.

Add salt and pepper to the flour; cover the pork before adding to a hot pan with melted butter until lightly browned.

Set the pork aside and keep warm.

In the same pan add a little butter (if required) and lightly brown the fennel.

Add the Marsala wine and stir before adding the stock; bring to the boil and reduce.

To roast the red pepper, cut the pepper into quarters and place in a bowl; cover with olive oil.

Place under a hot grill until the skins burn. Remove and cover with cling film, leave to stand. The skins will be easier to remove.

Cook the courgette in melted butter until golden. Add a little stock, the peppers, salt and pepper to taste and simmer.

To serve – serve 3 escalopes of pork, per person, on a warm plate with the courgette, pepper and a drizzle of Marsala sauce.

fillet of welsh beef in a whisky sauce

Serves 6
1.35kg/3 lbs of sirloin of Welsh beef
1.1 litres/2 pints of beef stock
175ml/6 fl oz of double cream
75g/3 oz of Welsh butter
3 shallots – finely chopped
1 tablespoon of olive oil
2 good measures of Welsh whisky
1–2 teaspoons of wholegrain mustard
sea salt and black pepper

meat

The potatoes
1.35 kg/3 lbs of new potatoes
6 tablespoons of olive oil
1 garlic bulb – separated into cloves
1 cabbage – thinly shredded
sea salt and black pepper

Method
Season the meat. Heat the oil in a roasting tin, and seal the meat
until browned.

Cook in a hot oven (200°C/Gas Mark 6) for 15 minutes
to each pound and an additional 15 minutes.

Melt the butter in a saucepan and fry the shallots until softened.

Add the whisky to the pan before adding the stock. Bring to the boil
and reduce.

Add the cream and mustard and cook until the sauce thickens.

Allow the meat to rest before carving.

The potatoes – Heat the oil in a large roasting tin. Add the new potatoes,
garlic and a good pinch of salt and pepper.

Roast at 200°C/Gas Mark 6 for approximately 15 minutes.

Cook the cabbage in butter for 2 minutes.

To serve – season, and serve the vegetables with the meat and the sauce.

steak and ale pies

Serves 6–8
450g/1 lb 2 oz of Welsh beef – cubed*
570ml/1 pint of beef stock
½ bottle of Brains SA beer
1 tablespoon of olive oil
1 tablespoon of tomato purée
2 teaspoons of English mustard
1 onion – finely chopped
1 packet of puff pastry
1 egg – beaten
flour – to roll out the pastry
sea salt and black pepper

Method

Season the meat and fry in the oil until browned.

Remove from the pan and set aside to rest.

In the same frying pan, fry the onions until soft, stir in the tomato purée and mustard and mix well.

Add the ale and stock and reduce before putting the meat back in the pan. Simmer for 1 hour or until the meat is tender.

Important! Cool the filling before filling the pastry.

Roll out a packet of puff pastry into thin layers. Cut out circles to fit a small pie tin, making sure you keep enough for the lids.

Fill the pastry with the meat filling, brush the egg over the lids and make small holes to allow to breathe.

Cook in a hot oven – 200°C/Gas Mark 6 for 20 minutes.

*The cooking time for the meat will vary, depending on the cut of meat you choose.

welsh lamb
with a laverbread stuffing

Serves 4

4 leg steaks of Welsh lamb

3 tablespoons of damson liqueur

1 lemon – rind and juice

1 tablespoon olive oil

Welsh butter– for frying

The stuffing

1 onion – finely chopped

bunch of fresh parsley – finely chopped

bunch of fresh sage – chopped

2 cloves of garlic – crushed

½ small loaf of breadcrumbs

1 beaten egg

1 tablespoon of fresh laverbread

4 tablespoons of oats

sea salt and black pepper

The sauce

6 damsons – stoned

2 glasses of red wine

1 tablespoon of balsamic vinegar

75ml/½ fl oz of single cream

Method

Remove the bone from the steaks. Season and marinade overnight with the damson liqueur, lemon juice and rind.

In a pan, heat the oil and butter and fry the steaks for 3–4 minutes until sealed.

Set aside in a roasting tin and reserve the juices for the sauce.

The stuffing – in a large bowl, mix the onion, parsley and sage before adding the breadcrumbs, garlic and laverbread. Beat the egg and mix into the ingredients and season well.

Mould the stuffing into small balls and coat with the oats.

Place the stuffing balls into the opening where the bone was removed. Roast in a hot oven (180°C/Gas Mark 4) for 15 minutes.

The sauce – add the meat juices to a hot frying pan and add the damsons, red wine and vinegar. Reduce before adding the cream, stir and simmer.

To serve – serve the steaks with a little sauce and fresh seasonal vegetables of your choice.

chilli

Serves 8–10

1.35 kg/3 lbs of Welsh beef – cut into cubes

500g/1 lb 2 oz of Pembrokeshire new potatoes – uncooked and halved

2 tins of tomatoes – chopped

2 large tins of red kidney beans

4 red chillies, deseeded – finely chopped

4 cloves of garlic – finely chopped

2 onions – cut into cubes

2 beef stock cubes

1 tablespoon of tomato purée

2 teaspoons of paprika

2 teaspoons of cumin powder

1 litre/2 pints of water

2 tablespoons of chilli powder

2 tablespoons of brown sugar

olive oil, juice of ½ lime, sea salt and black pepper

Method

In a large saucepan, brown the beef in the oil.

Add a pinch each of black pepper, paprika, chilli powder and the stock cubes, and mix well.

Add the onions and the garlic and cook until brown.

Mix in the purée and cook for a few minutes before adding the sugar, tomatoes, chillies, cumin and the water.

Mix well and bring to the boil and leave to simmer on a medium heat for 1 hour.

Add the potatoes and beans and simmer for a further 30 minutes.

Before serving add the lime juice.

To serve – serve with rice or chunks of fresh bread, a spoonful of sour cream and fresh coriander.

lamb steaks and marinade

Serves 4

4 Welsh lamb steaks

The marinade

3 cloves of garlic

2 onions – cubed

1 tablespoon of balsamic vinegar

1 pot of plain yoghurt

1 teaspoon of chilli powder

juice of lemon

½ teaspoon of coriander

½ teaspoon of ginger

½ teaspoon of cumin

½ teaspoon of turmeric

sea salt

Method

Place all the ingredients in a food processor and mix until smooth.

Pour the marinade over the meat, place in the refrigerator and allow to stand overnight.

Heat the grill or a barbecue and cook the meat for approximately 8 minutes each side (according to weight and to your taste).

preseli lamb

Serves 4–6

shoulder of Preseli lamb (boned and quartered)

2 teaspoons of paprika

1 tablespoon of olive oil

a good pinch of cumin seeds

5 cloves of garlic – thinly sliced

The sauce

1.1 litres/2 pints of hot lamb stock

3 stalks of celery – sliced

3 carrots – finely chopped

2 tablespoons of olive oil

1 onion – finely chopped

2 tablespoons of tomato purée

handful of fresh coriander – finely chopped

½ bottle of good red wine, rind of ½ lemon

Method

In a frying pan, seal the meat using a little of the oil. Season with salt, pepper and the paprika and add the cumin seeds and garlic to the meat and brown.

Set the meat aside.

The sauce – using the same frying pan as the meat was cooked in, mix the tomato purée with the pieces of meat that are left in the pan. Then add the wine and reduce. Add the stock and simmer for approximately 5 minutes.

Stir the coriander and lemon rind into the sauce. In a deep pan, melt the vegetables in oil and leave to sweat under a lid for approximately 3–4 minutes.

Place the pieces of meat on top of the vegetables and pour the sauce on top. Cook at 160°C/Gas Mark 2 for two hours.

Once the meat has been cooked, liquidize the vegetables to create a smooth sauce.

To serve – serve with vegetables of your choice.

sausage and bean casserole

Serves 8
900g/2 lb of fresh pork sausages – two per person
1 tin of cannellini beans
1 tin of butter beans
1 tin of borlotti beans
1 tin of tomatoes
1 bottle of good red wine
570ml/1 pint of pork or chicken stock
225g/8 oz of dried apricots – finely chopped
2–4 small red chillies – finely chopped
3 cloves of garlic – finely chopped
2 pieces of celery – finely chopped
1 tablespoon of tomato purée
2 apples – peeled and chopped
1 onion – thinly sliced
handful of fresh rosemary – finely chopped
2 tablespoons of olive oil
sea salt and black pepper

Method
In a frying pan, brown the sausages. Set aside.

In the same pan, fry the onions, garlic, celery, tomato purée and a little salt and pepper and brown them for a few minutes.

Add the red wine, rosemary and chillies and leave to boil until they have reduced to a thick sauce.

Transfer everything into a large saucepan and add the tomatoes, apples, stock and beans and mix well. Put the sausages into the saucepan with the apricots and mix together.

Cook all ingredients on a low heat for 1–1½ hours.

To serve – serve with mashed potatoes.

game meatloaf

Serves 4–6

1 round white loaf

2 goose breasts

2 pieces of chicken

3 large mushrooms

3 rashers of bacon

1 red onion – thinly sliced

1 red pepper and 1 yellow pepper – roasted and skinned

1 small leek – steamed

4 tablespoons of olive oil

juice of 1 lemon, pinch of sugar, fresh basil leaves, sea salt and black pepper

Method

Cut the top off the bread and set aside. Carefully remove the bread from the middle of the loaf without damaging the crust or making holes in it.

Heat the oil in a large pan. Put salt and pepper on the pieces of chicken and goose and cook in the oil for 8–10 minutes. Be careful not to overcook.

Lift the poultry from the pan and set aside. Leave the juices in the pan.

Using the same pan, gently fry the bacon and onions in the juices.

Add some more oil, put in the mushrooms and cook for around 8 minutes. Add the lemon juice, sugar and salt and pepper. Reserve the juice.

To build the loaf – place a piece of chicken, bacon and goose in the loaf followed by pieces of red and yellow pepper, onions, leek and one big mushroom.

Repeat and keep building until the loaf is nearly full then pour the juices from the pan all over the meat and vegetables before sealing with the top of the bread.

Wrap in foil and leave overnight in the fridge with plenty of weight on top (you could use two cartons of orange juice).

To serve – remove the foil and cut the loaf into thick slices. Serve with fresh salad.

welsh lamb and potato tart

Serves 8

2–3kg/6 lbs shoulder of Welsh lamb

2kg/4 lbs 6 oz of Maris Piper potatoes – peeled and thickly sliced (uncooked)

200ml/7 fl oz of chicken stock

100ml/3½ fl oz of Welsh white wine

20g/1 oz of parsley – finely chopped

6 sprigs of rosemary – 3 whole, 3 finely chopped

1 or 2 bulbs of garlic

olive oil

Llangadog butter

sea salt and black pepper

Method

Heat a roasting tin containing some olive oil.

Rub the lamb with garlic and plenty of seasoning.

Seal the meat in the tin until lightly browned.

Add the white wine, and 3 or 4 sprigs of rosemary.

Cover the meat with foil and bake at a low heat, 140–150°C/Gas Mark 1–2, for 6 hours.

When the meat is cooked, it will come off the bone easily enough. Retain the juices in the roasting tin to make stock. (Leftover meat from the Sunday joint can also be used.)

Rub garlic over a 5cm/2" deep ovenproof dish, and place a layer of potatoes in the dish until the base is covered.

Season and sprinkle rosemary and parsley over the top.

Place a layer of lamb over the potatoes to a thickness of around 1.25cm/½". Repeat this process.

Finally, place a double layer of potatoes on top and add more salt, pepper, rosemary and parsley.

Pour the stock over the tart, letting it soak in.

Cover the dish and bake in the oven at 180°C/Gas Mark 4 for approximately 1¼ hours.

Leave to cool and refrigerate for at least 8 hours.

To serve – spread a mixture of oil and butter over the tart and warm it in a hot oven for 20–25 minutes until the potatoes have browned.

thai lamb casserole with lime and coriander dumplings

1.1kg/2¾ lbs of lamb – cut into large chunks

2 tins of coconut milk

2 teaspoons of vegetable oil

2 onions – cut into cubes

4 cloves of garlic

3 red peppers – cut into cubes

2.5cm/1" piece of fresh ginger – finely chopped

1 stem of lemon grass – finely crushed

2 hot chillies – finely chopped

50g/2 oz of palm sugar or brown sugar

1.1 litres/2 pints of lamb stock

2 tablespoons of nam pla

zest of 1 orange

2 tablespoons of tomato purée

bunch of fresh coriander – finely chopped

Lime and Coriander Dumplings

275g/10 oz of plain flour

110g/4 oz of suet

zest of 2 limes

bunch of coriander – finely chopped

½ an onion – finely chopped

125ml/4 fl oz of milk

1 egg – beaten

sea salt and black pepper

Method

Heat the oil in a large casserole dish.

Rub salt and black pepper into the meat, place in the casserole dish and brown slowly.

Lift out the meat, place in a bowl and leave to one side.

Put the onions and garlic into the casserole and fry gently for two minutes before adding the red pepper, ginger, lemon grass and chillies and cook until browned. Finally, add the stock, nam pla, tomato purée, sugar, orange zest and the pieces of lamb and mix well. Place in a preheated oven at 180°C/Gas Mark 4 for 1½ hours.

The Lime and Coriander Dumplings – in a large bowl mix together the suet, flour, salt and black pepper, onion, lime zest and coriander. Then add the milk and the egg. Mix it all together to form a thick mix which can be shaped into balls similar in size to golf balls.

After the casserole has cooked for 1½ hours remove it from the oven and add the coconut milk. Stir it in and leave to simmer on the hob for 10–15 minutes, until it thickens.

Then add the dumplings and half the coriander to the casserole and return to the oven to cook for a further 20 minutes.

To serve – serve with the remaining fresh coriander.

pork in mead sauce
with sage and honey cakes

Serves 2
2 pork chops
70ml/½ fl oz of mead
70ml/½ fl oz of pork stock
50g/2 oz of butter
8–10 white mushrooms – chopped into small pieces
1 shallot – finely chopped
2 tablespoons of whipping cream
½ teaspoon of paprika powder, sea salt and black pepper

The cakes
½ an onion – finely chopped
1 clove of garlic – minced
bunch of fresh parsley – finely chopped
2 tablespoons of sage leaves – finely chopped
½ a white loaf, crumbed
1 teaspoon of Welsh honey
50g/2 oz melted butter
sea salt and black pepper

Method
Rub the paprika, salt and black pepper into the meat.

Heat a frying pan and melt half the butter. Cook both sides of the meat until brown. Add the shallot and cook until soft before adding the mushrooms and browning lightly.

Pour the mead and the stock over the mixture and simmer to reduce to half its original quantity. To finish the sauce, add the cream and remaining butter and warm through.

The cakes – mix all the ingredients in a bowl to make a light dough.

Shape the dough into small balls and cook in a frying pan or in the oven until browned.

chicken

cold chicken curry

Serves 4–6

The stock
1 whole chicken
1 onion – cubed
1 stick of celery – sliced
1 carrot – sliced
2 teaspoons of cumin
1 bay leaf
sea salt and black pepper
flour to thicken

The curry
2 red chillies – chopped
2 cloves of garlic – chopped
1 tablespoon of sesame oil
1 onion – sliced
1 small jar of mayonnaise
2.5cm/1" piece of ginger – peeled and chopped
½ tin of coconut milk
green curry paste
½ tablespoon of Thai fish sauce (nam pla)
1 bunch of coriander– chopped
zest of 1 orange

Method

The stock – place the chicken in large saucepan with onion, celery, carrot, bay leaf, cumin, salt and pepper.

Bring to the boil then simmer for required time – 20 minutes to the pound.

Remove chicken from the saucepan and leave to cool.

Reduce the chicken stock and blend all ingredients in saucepan.

Thicken and leave to cool.

The curry – in a large wok, heat the sesame oil, fry the cubed onion until soft and add garlic, ginger and chilli and cook for 3–5 minutes.

Mix in the green curry paste and fish sauce and stir well before adding the coconut milk. Bring to the boil and reduce by half. Leave to cool.

When cool, place in a large mixing bowl with fresh coriander, zest of orange and the jar of mayonnaise.

When chicken is cold, remove all meat off the bone and break up into bite-sized pieces.

Place in the bowl with curry mix.

Add required amount of thickened stock to chilled curry, mix together and chill before serving.

chicken balls in a tomato sauce

Serves 4–6

The chicken
450g/1 lb of chicken – minced
1 onion – very finely chopped
2 tablespoons of tomato purée
1 egg, beaten
olive oil
large sprig of sage
plain flour – to roll the balls

The sauce
570ml/1 pint of chicken stock
1 onion – finely chopped
2 tablespoons of tomato purée
1 tin of tomatoes
olive oil

Method
The sauce – in a saucepan or deep frying pan, fry the onions in the oil. Add the tomato purée and fry until brown.

Pour in the stock and the tomatoes and leave to reduce for 10 minutes.

The chicken – fry the onions in the oil and leave to cool.

In a large bowl, mix the minced chicken with the onions, the sage and salt and pepper. Add an egg to bind the ingredients together.

Mix well before shaping into small balls.

Roll the balls in the flour and fry until brown.

Transfer the chicken balls to the tomato sauce and simmer for 5 minutes.

To serve – serve with a mountain of mashed potatoes or pasta.

chicken curry

Serves 4

4 pieces of chicken – cut into strips

The marinade

275ml/½ pint of yoghurt

50g/2 oz of tomato purée

25g/1 oz of Madras curry paste

3 cloves of garlic – crushed to a paste

1 tablespoon of olive oil

2 green chillies – finely chopped

juice of two lemons

1 teaspoon of ginger powder

1 teaspoon of cumin powder

1 teaspoon of coriander powder

handful of fresh coriander – finely chopped

handful of fresh mint – finely chopped

The sauce

350g/12 oz of tinned tomatoes – finely chopped

275ml/½ pint of water

4 red chillies – finely chopped

3 cloves of garlic

1 tablespoon of oil

1–2 teaspoons of sugar

2.5cm/1" piece of fresh ginger – peeled and crushed to a paste

1 teaspoon of chilli powder

1 teaspoon of dried chillies

2 tablespoons of tomato purée

1 teaspoon of turmeric

1 teaspoon of coriander powder

1 teaspoon of garam massala

1 teaspoon of cumin powder

2 tablespoons of Madras curry paste

Method

Mix all the marinade ingredients in a bowl except for the chicken.

Add the meat to the marinade and leave in the fridge overnight.

Heat a little oil in a frying pan and cook the pieces of meat (they could also be cooked under a hot grill or on a barbecue).

The chicken can be eaten with some salad, without the sauce.

The sauce – heat the oil in a saucepan or deep frying pan. Add the paste, garlic and ginger and heat them before adding the chilli powder and dried chillies and cook for approximately 2 minutes.

Then add the tomato purée, turmeric, coriander, garam massala and cumin and cook on a low heat for 5 minutes taking care not to burn them.

Finally, add the tomatoes, water, sugar, chillies and a spoonful of Madras paste and simmer on a low heat for an hour.

Add the chicken to the saucepan approximately 5 minutes before the hour comes to an end for the chicken to cook through.

To serve – serve with rice.

chicken couscous

Serves 4
2 chicken breasts – sliced diagonally
275ml/½ pint of chicken stock
250g/9 oz of couscous
1 tablespoon of sesame oil
2 cloves of garlic – crushed
1 red pepper and, 1 yellow pepper – diced and deseeded
1 red onion – diced
1 courgette – sliced lengthways, diced and deseeded
1 small punnet of baby tomatoes – halved
2.5cm/1" piece of ginger – finely chopped
handful of fresh basil – chopped
handful of parsley – chopped
zest of ½ a lemon
olive oil
sea salt and black pepper

Method
Place the couscous in a large bowl.

Add the stock – sufficient to cover the couscous – and leave for 15 minutes. When the couscous has absorbed the stock, add 2 tablespoons of olive oil and mix well.

In a frying pan, heat the sesame oil and 1 tablespoon of olive oil and fry the onion, one clove of garlic and the ginger.

To the onion mixture, add the red pepper, yellow pepper and courgette and fry for 2–3 minutes.

In another frying pan, heat 2 tablespoons of olive oil and fry the chicken and garlic.

Add the chicken and the vegetables to the couscous, then the basil, parsley, tomatoes and lemon zest.

Mix until well combined and season to taste.

To serve – serve hot or cold.

chicken with ginger and lime

Serves 4–6
1 fresh chicken (1.35–2.25kg/3–5 lbs)
1 onion – halved
2 limes
1 clove of garlic – thinly sliced
5cm/2" piece of fresh ginger – skinned and thinly sliced
2 tablespoons of olive oil or butter
sea salt and black pepper

Method

Whilst preparing the chicken, preheat the oven to 160°C/Gas Mark 2.

With a sharp knife, cut into the meat about ½" deep. Put six of these cuts on each breast and four in both legs.

Peel the zest from one of the limes.

Push pieces of garlic, ginger and lime zest into the cuts.

Squeeze the lime juices over the meat.

Place the chicken in a roasting tin and push the onion halves and the remaining ginger, garlic and lime into the cavity.

Rub the olive oil over the chicken before sprinkling salt and black pepper over it.

Roast in the oven for 20 minutes per pound and another 20 minutes at 160°C/Gas Mark 2.

To serve – Serve hot or cold.

pesto chicken and potato salad

Serves 4

500g/1 lb 2 oz of new potatoes – unpeeled
110g/4 oz of baby spinach leaves
3 chicken breasts – skinned, cooked and cut into chunks
3 tablespoons of olive oil
1 tablespoon of pesto
juice of 1 lemon
sea salt and black pepper

Method

Boil the potatoes in salted water for 15 minutes.

Drain and return to the pan, and roughly crush with a fork.

Add the chunks of chicken to the pan then the spinach leaves.

Mix gently, using a large spoon or your hands.

Finally add the pesto, lemon juice and oil to the other ingredients, and toss to coat everything in the dressing.

Season to taste.

pasta and rice

wild mushrooms ravioli

Serves 4

The pasta
250g/9 oz of plain flour
3 egg yolks
1 tablespoon of olive oil
a drop of water
a pinch of salt

The filling
200g/7 oz of wild mushrooms –
    washed and cubed
50g/2 oz of small white mushrooms
25g/1 oz of butter
1 shallot – finely chopped
juice of ¼ lemon
salt and pepper

The sauce
1 shallot – finely chopped
100g/3½ oz of button mushrooms – trimmed and finely chopped
25g/1 oz of cold butter
100g/3½ oz of wild mushrooms
100ml/3½ fl oz of dry Alsace wine
500ml/18 fl oz of chicken stock (or vegetable stock for vegetarians)
3 tablespoons of double cream
25g/¾ oz of cold butter – diced
salt and pepper
dash of lemon juice

Method

In a food processor, mix the flour, egg yolks, water, oil and salt until crumbed.

Work the crumbs with your hands until a smooth dough is formed.

Wrap in cling film and allow to stand in a fridge for 1 hour.

The filling – sweat the shallots in butter for 1 minute until transparent, add the mushrooms and cook over a high heat, stirring continuously for 2 minutes.

Remove from the heat, then season with salt and pepper and a dash of lemon juice.

Cool on a piece of kitchen paper allowing any moisture in the mushrooms to drain away.

The sauce – sweat the shallots in butter without colouring, add the mushrooms and sweat gently for 2 minutes, stirring from time to time.

Add the wine and reduce by two-thirds. Add the water and cream and whisk in the cold diced butter until the sauce is well-emulsified.

Taste, season and add a dash of lemon juice.

Liquidise and strain the sauce, pressing with a ladle to extract as much sauce as possible. Reserve in a small saucepan.

Reserve the mushrooms and mix with the filling.

Once the dough has chilled, work it through a pasta-rolling machine to create a thin smooth layer of pasta.

Cut the pasta into circles and add a spoonful of filling to the centre of each circle.

Fold the pasta over the filling and seal with a little water to form a ravioli parcel.

Bring a saucepan of lightly salted water to the boil and poach the ravioli in the water for precisely 2 minutes.

To serve – place the ravioli parcels on a bed of spinach quickly fried in butter, and pour the sauce over.

saffron rice

Serves 4

200g/7 oz of Basmati rice – washed and soaked in salted water
    for 3 hours
80g/3 oz of unsalted butter
5 whole green cardamom pods – cracked
½ cinnamon stick
1 clove of garlic
3 whole black peppercorns – crushed
1 tablespoon of chopped pistachio nuts
1 tablespoon of raisins
1 good pinch of saffron threads – infused in 4 tablespoons of
    boiling water
sea salt

To serve

200g/7 oz of Greek yoghurt
1 clove of garlic – crushed
sea salt and black pepper

Method

Melt the butter in a large saucepan.

Add the garlic, cinnamon, cardamom pods and black peppercorns and fry on a low heat for approximately 4 minutes.

Drain the rice, add to the butter and stir to coat for a minute.

Turn up the heat, stir in the pistachios, raisins and saffron and pour enough water over the rice to cover. Season with salt; place some greaseproof paper on the surface and place a lid on the saucepan. Bring to the boil and simmer for 5 minutes.

Remove the paper and drizzle the saffron water evenly over the rice. Replace the paper and lid.

Turn down the heat (medium to low) and cook for another 4–5 minutes.

Add the garlic and seasoning to the yoghurt. Serve as an accompaniment.

spaghetti and chicken arrabiata

Serves 2
2 pieces of chicken breast, sliced
3 tablespoons of olive oil
1 onion – finely chopped
1 clove of garlic
1 large red chilli – finely chopped
2 small red chillies – finely chopped
2 tablespoons of tomato purée
1 large tin of tomatoes – chopped
spaghetti (enough for 2 people)
sea salt and black pepper

To serve
basil leaves
Parmesan cheese

Method
In a frying pan, heat the oil and lightly brown the onions and garlic.

Add the chillies and tomato purée and cook until a rich red colour.

Add the tomatoes and a little salt to taste and simmer for approximately 5 minutes.

Cook the spaghetti in a large pan of boiling water until *al dente* (8–10 minutes).

In another frying pan, heat the olive oil and fry the pieces of chicken, then add salt and pepper to taste.

Add the spaghetti to the chicken, mix in the arrabiata sauce and serve with fresh basil and Parmesan cheese.

summer vegetable risotto

Serves 4
500g/1 lb 2 oz of Arborio rice
450g/1 lb of fresh peas
100g/3½ oz of butter
100g/3½ oz of Parmesan cheese – grated
1.5 litres/2½ pints of vegetable stock
275ml/½ pint of double cream
100ml/3½ fl oz of white wine (not too dry)
2 shallots – finely chopped
1 bunch of asparagus
1 courgette – deseeded, and cut at an angle
1 packet of mangetout – cut into thin strips
1 bunch of parsley – chopped
zest of 1 lemon
sea salt and black pepper

Method

In a large frying pan, melt the butter over a low heat and fry the shallots.

Add the rice and heat through in the butter.

Add the wine and stir before adding the stock; turn up the heat.

Mix well after adding salt, pepper and lemon zest and cook until the rice thickens and absorbs all the liquid. Add the courgettes, cleaned and chopped asparagus stems and mix well. Add the cream, Parmesan and mangetout, and stir before adding the asparagus tips, fresh peas, lemon zest and parsley.

Heat through before serving.

tuna and pasta bake

Serves 4–6

1 onion – finely chopped
2 carrots – thinly sliced
½ broccoli – separated into small florets
6 mushrooms – thinly sliced
1 large tin of tuna
30g/1 oz of cooked pasta of your choice
30g/1 oz of fresh breadcrumbs
sea salt and black pepper

The béchamel sauce

570ml/1 pint of whole milk
50g/2 oz of plain flour
50g/2 oz of butter
50g/2 oz of grated cheese of your choice
pinch of nutmeg
1 teaspoon of English mustard powder

Method

Prepare the béchamel sauce in a saucepan by melting the butter on a medium heat and mixing in the flour.

Add the milk a little at a time and mix until smooth.

Add the cheese, nutmeg, mustard powder and salt and pepper to taste.

In a large lasagne dish, place a layer of onions, carrots, broccoli and mushrooms.

Add a layer of tuna and cooked pasta on top.

Pour the sauce over the top before adding a sprinkling of breadcrumbs.

Bake in the oven at 180°C/Gas Mark 4 for 30 minutes until brown.

To serve – serve with vegetables of your choice.

bulgar wheat salad

Serves 4

350g/12 oz of Bulgar wheat

225g/½ lb of fresh peas – cooked

425ml/¾ pint of hot vegetable stock

2 red onions – diced

2 cloves of garlic – finely chopped

1 red chilli – finely chopped

2 tablespoons of honey

2 tablespoons of olive oil

zest of 1 lime

1 bunch of spring onions – chopped

1 bunch of fresh mint – chopped

sea salt and black pepper

Method

Place the Bulgar wheat in a large mixing bowl and cover with enough hot stock (enough to cover the Bulgar wheat).

Leave until the wheat has absorbed all the stock (approximately 15–20 minutes).

Heat the oil in a pan, add the onions, garlic and chilli, and fry until softened.

Add the honey, zest of lime, spring onions and peas, stir and heat through.

Add the warm ingredients to the Bulgar wheat, then mix well before adding the fresh mint.

Season with salt and pepper to taste.

Serve hot or cold.

tuna pasta nicoise

Serves 4

350g/12 oz of pasta

2 tablespoons of olive oil

½ tablespoon of lemon juice

½ tablespoon of white wine vinegar

300g/10 oz of cherry tomatoes – halved

50g/2 oz can of anchovies – drained and chopped

200g/7 oz can of tuna in water – drained and broken
into chunks

a bunch each of fresh basil and parsley –
finely chopped

sea salt and black pepper

Method

Cook the pasta in a pan of boiling salted water for 10–12 minutes or according to the instructions.

In a pan with a lid, heat the oil, lemon juice and vinegar, adding the tomatoes and anchovies then cover and gently warm through until the tomatoes just start to burst and soften.

Drain the pasta and return it to pan.

Add the tuna to the pasta before adding the tomato sauce and the herbs.

Season with freshly ground black pepper.

Serve immediately.

vegetables

ratatouille

Serves 4–6

8 fresh tomatoes – skinned, deseeded and cut into quarters
6 spring onions – finely chopped
3 courgettes
1 tablespoon of tomato purée
2 tablespoons of olive oil
1 onion – chopped into chunks
2 cloves of garlic
1 aubergine
1 red pepper – cubed
1 yellow pepper – cubed
1 bunch of coriander – finely chopped
sea salt and black pepper

Method

In a large frying pan fry the onions and garlic in the oil for approximately
3–4 minutes until soft.

Cut the aubergine lengthways into four and remove the seeds and cube.
Cut the courgette likewise.

Add the aubergine and courgette to the frying pan.

Add the salt, pepper and tomato purée and brown before adding the peppers.

Cook together for a further 3–4 minutes.

Place the tomatoes in a large bowl and add the ingredients from the frying
pan, together with the spring onions and coriander. You could add a little
balsamic vinegar if desired.

Mix well before serving.

Serve hot or cold.

pembrokeshire new potatoes dauphinoise

Serves 4–6
450g/1 lb of Pembrokeshire new potatoes
1 onion – sliced
Welsh butter – for frying
2 cloves of garlic
1 leek – thinly sliced
570ml/1 pint of double cream
1 large Camembert cheese – sliced
1 bunch of fresh parsley, sea salt and black pepper

Method

Boil the potatoes and leave to cool before crushing them with your hands.

In a frying pan, heat the butter, add the onions and garlic and soften.

Add the double cream and heat gently.

Add the potatoes to the cream and heat through.

In a frying pan heat the butter and gently fry the leek with a little black pepper to taste.

To finish the dish, build layers of the potato mixture, leek mixture and Camembert in an ovenproof dish.

Top with a sprinkling of fresh parsley.

Cook in a preheated oven at a temperature of 180–200°C/Gas Mark 5 for 20 minutes.

spicy potato wedges

Serves 4
8–12 white potatoes – washed but not peeled
1 tablespoon of olive oil
1 teaspoon of paprika
1 teaspoon of mixed dried herbs
sea salt and black pepper

Method
Cut the potatoes into quarters and place in a baking tray.

Pour some olive oil over the potatoes, then the paprika, herbs and a good pinch of salt and pepper.

Cook at 200°C/Gas Mark 6 for 15–20 minutes until nicely browned and crisp.

cheese, leek and potato cakes

Serves 4
700g/1½ lbs of potatoes (Desirée, King Edward or Maris Piper)
olive oil
50g/2 oz of Welsh butter
100g/3½ oz of Emmenthal cheese – grated
50g/2 oz of Gorgonzola cheese – cut into pieces
2 leeks – finely chopped
3 egg yolks
sea salt and black pepper

Method
Peel, boil and mash the potatoes.

In a frying pan, melt some of the butter and fry the leeks lightly with some black pepper.

In a bowl, mix the mashed potatoes, leeks, Emmenthal and Gorgonzola cheese, a little more butter and salt and pepper with the egg yolks.

Mix well and shape into potato cakes.

Heat the olive oil in a frying pan and fry the potato cakes on both sides until they are lightly browned.

broad beans with black pudding

Serves 4

500g/1 lb of broad beans – podded weight
200g/7 oz of black pudding – cut 1–2cm thick
100ml/3 fl oz of chicken stock
3 tablespoons of olive oil
2 cloves of garlic – thinly sliced
bunch of fresh mint – roughly chopped
½ teaspoon of fennel seeds
sea salt and black pepper

Method

In a frying pan, heat the olive oil and add the black pudding. Fry until browned on both sides, trying not to let the black pudding break up too much.

Remove from pan and set aside. Add the garlic and fennel seeds and fry for a minute until the garlic begins to colour, being careful not to burn it.

Add the broad beans, some pepper, stock and mint and cook for 3–4 minutes until the beans are cooked.

Return the black pudding to the pan on top of the beans, heat for about 5 minutes and stir in the mint.

Season with salt and pepper and serve immediately.

roasted cherry tomatoes

450g/1 lb of cherry tomatoes
½ litre/17½ fl oz of olive oil
2 onions – thinly sliced
1 clove of garlic
1 bunch of fresh thyme
2 tablespoons of sea salt
black pepper

Method

Heat the olive oil in a frying pan and fry the onions and garlic until soft.

Add the tomatoes and thyme and roast in the oven at 200°C /Gas Mark 6 for 20 minutes (keeping the tomatoes whole).

Leave the tomatoes to cool in the oil before pouring into a large jar to store in the fridge.

asparagus and parma ham rolls

Serves 4–6
1 bunch of fresh asparagus
4–6 slices of Carmarthenshire ham or Parma ham
4 tablespoons of walnut oil
1 tablespoon of balsamic vinegar
sea salt and black pepper

Method

Fold the asparagus about an inch from the bottom and then cut off the tough base segment. You will only need to use the top piece (retain the tough base segment to use in soup).

Cook the asparagus in salted water for around 4 minutes. Leave to cool.

Wrap the ham around each piece of the asparagus.

The sauce – in a clean lidded jam jar (or similar), combine together the walnut oil, balsamic vinegar, salt and pepper.

Before serving, pour the sauce over the asparagus.

vegetarian

italian bruschetta

Serves 8
1 French stick
olive oil
8 fresh tomatoes – deseeded and finely chopped
handful of fresh basil – finely chopped
1 red onion – finely chopped
2–3 cloves of garlic – finely chopped
juice of 1 lemon
1 pack of Mozzarella cheese – cut into 8 slices
salt and black pepper

Method

Cut the bread into thick slices, drizzle with olive oil, and season.

Cook in a hot oven for 10 minutes.

In a large mixing bowl, mix the tomatoes, onions, garlic, basil, lemon juice, some olive oil and salt and pepper.

Put the mixture on the bread and place a slice of mozzarella on top to finish.

Place in the oven or under a hot grill to melt the cheese.

Serve whilst hot.

muska boreau

Serves 4–6
1 200g/7 oz pack of feta cheese – crumbled
1 pack of filo pastry
1 pack of spinach
handful of fresh dill – finely chopped
butter – melted
olive oil
flour – to roll the dough
salt and pepper

Method

In a pan, cook the spinach in a little oil and salt and pepper for 2 minutes.

In a bowl, mix the cheese, dill and salt and pepper.

Spread a little of the melted butter onto a layer of filo pastry before placing another layer on top.

Place a generous spoonful of the mixture on top and fold to form a triangular shape.

Cook in the oven at 160°C/Gas Mark 2 for 10 minutes, until a light golden colour.

blue cheese soufflé

Serves 4

20g/1 oz of butter
20g/1 oz of plain flour
20g/1 oz o Dolcelatte cheese – cut into four pieces
50ml/2 fl oz milk
30g/1½ oz of Camembert cheese – diced
pinch of salt to taste
pinch of cayenne pepper
pinch of black pepper
1 egg yolk
3 egg whites
juice of ¼ of a lemon

To line the moulds
butter
12g/½ oz breadcrumbs
4g/¼ oz hazelnuts – chopped

Method

Make a béchamel sauce (see page 84) with the butter, flour and milk then add the Camembert.

Mix well until the cheese is absorbed, leaving a smooth sauce.

Allow to cool before adding the egg yolk, cayenne pepper, salt and pepper. Mix well.

Lightly butter the ramekins inside, then line with hazelnuts and breadcrumbs.

Beat the egg whites with a squeeze of lemon juice until the whites reach full peak.

Fill the ramekins with the soufflé mixture one third up, add the diced Dolcelatte, cover with the mixture and smooth the surface.

Line a suitable Bain–Marie with paper and fill with water to a depth of 1cm.

Place the ramekins in the tray, bring the water to the boil, then place into the oven and bake at 190°C/Gas Mark 5 for 10 minutes.

Carefully remove the soufflés from their moulds; the soufflés may be kept for several hours at this stage.

To reheat, place in a very hot oven (220°C/Gas Mark 7) for 5 minutes to give them a crust.

welsh rarebit
with poached pears

Serves 6
450g/1 lb strong Cheddar cheese, grated
40ml/1 fl oz mild ale
2 pinches ground paprika
1 large egg
1 teaspoon hot mustard
1 teaspoon Worcestershire sauce

The pears
6 pears, peeled
1 bottle of red wine
1 split vanilla pod
2 star anise
zest of half an orange
4 tablespoons soft brown sugar
1 hot red chilli, split in half

Method

In a large bowl combine the cheese, egg, mustard, sauce, paprika and ale together well. Leave to stand in the refrigerator for one hour.

In a large pan bring the red wine, vanilla pod, star anise, orange zest and brown sugar to the boil. Place the pears in the pan and simmer on low heat for around 40 minutes. The pears will soften slightly as they cook.

Allow to cool, then refrigerate.

Carefully cut the pears in half lengthways and remove the seeds. Fill with a generous spoonful of the cheese mixture.

Place under a moderate grill until the pears are warm and the cheese is melted and browned.

laverbread, ricotta and spinach pancakes

Serves 4

The pancakes
100g/4 oz plain flour
50g/2 oz laverbread
10g/½ oz melted butter
275ml/½ pint milk
1 large egg
a pinch of salt

The filling
450g/1 lb young spinach leaves
150g/5 oz ricotta cheese
50g/2 oz Parmesan cheese
50g/2 oz butter
1 large egg
1 clove of garlic, crushed
½ tsp freshly-grated nutmeg
zest of half a lemon
sea salt and pepper

The tomato sauce
50g/2 oz butter
2 cloves of garlic, crushed
2 tablespoons tomato purée
glass of white wine
half an onion, finely chopped
sea salt and pepper

laverbread, ricotta and spinach pancakes

Method

Prepare the béchamel sauce in advance (see page 84).

The pancakes – beat the eggs and milk together. Sift the flour and salt into the mixture. Gradually add the milk and eggs, beating well to prevent lumps.

Mix the laverbread into the mixture before adding the butter.

Leave to stand in the refrigerator for an hour.

The filling – melt the butter and fry the garlic until lightly browned. Add the spinach and cook for 1–2 minutes. Discard the liquid from the pan. Cool the spinach mixture on a plate.

In a bowl, mix the ricotta cheese, the egg, the Parmesan cheese, the nutmeg, lemon zest and the spinach, and season to taste.

The sauce – fry the onions and garlic in the butter.

Add the tomato purée and cook for 2 minutes.

Add the wine and reduce the sauce before adding the tomatoes and seasoning, and cook for half an hour on a low heat.

Cook the pancakes on both sides in a pan until lightly browned.

Place two tablespoons of the cheese filling in the centre of each pancake and fold the sides to form a closed parcel, taking care that none of the filling escapes.

Place the pancakes in an ovenproof dish. Pour the tomato sauce over the pancakes, followed by the Béchamel sauce.

Finally, sprinkle the pancakes with a little Parmesan cheese and bake in the oven at 180°C/Gas Mark 4 for 20 minutes.

tomato and olive tartlets

Serves 4–6
1 pack of puff pastry
olive oil
10 fresh tomatoes – plum or on the vine – each cut into eight pieces
2 onions, thinly sliced
4 cloves of garlic, crushed
2 tablespoons of tomato purée
20 black olives
1 bunch fresh basil
175g/6 oz Gruyère or Emmenthal cheese, grated

Method
Roll out the pastry thinly and cut 4–6 fairly large circles (use the lid of a small saucepan). Let the pastry rest before you use it.

Heat the oil in a frying pan and fry the onions and garlic for two minutes. Add the tomato purée and fry for a further two minutes.

Add the tomatoes and a pinch of salt and pepper, then allow to cool (a pinch of sugar may be required to improve the taste of the tomatoes).

Spread the tomato mixture onto the pastry circles.

Divide the olives and the basil leaves evenly between them before covering them with the cheese.

Bake in the oven for 10–15 minutes on 180°C/Gas Mark 4 until the cheese has melted and the pastry has risen.

desserts

banana, rum and yoghurt

Serves 4
50g/2 oz of butter
6 bananas, cut at an angle
1 tablespoon of brown sugar
a good measure of rum
zest of 1 lemon

To serve
cream or Greek yoghurt

Method
In a large frying pan, melt the butter. Add the bananas and cook until golden brown.

Melt the sugar before adding the rum and flambé the mixture.

To finish, stir in the zest of the lemon.

To serve – serve with fresh cream or Greek yoghurt.

bara brith pudding

Serves 6–8
Loaf of bara brith – sliced into 12 pieces
50g/2 oz of Welsh unsalted butter

The custard
8 egg yolks
75g/6 oz of caster sugar
1 vanilla pod
300ml/½ pt of milk
300ml/½ pt of double cream

Method
Butter the bara brith slices and cut in half. Arrange the bara brith slices in an ovenproof dish or individual ramekins. Put one unbuttered slice aside.

The custard – whisk the egg yolks and gradually add the caster sugar.

In a saucepan, split the vanilla pod and add to the milk and cream; simmer and leave to cool.

Pour the mixture through a sieve, stirring vigorously all the time to form a custard.

Pour the custard mixture over the bara brith. Then place the unbuttered slice on top.

Cook slowly in a roasting tin half-filled with water at 160°C/Gas Mark 2 for approximately 30–45 minutes.

To serve – dust with sieved icing sugar.

brandy snap baskets

Serves 4
125g/4½ oz of butter
125g/4½ oz of light brown sugar
125g/4½ oz of golden syrup
125g/4½ oz of plain flour
4 teaspoons of lemon juice
1 teaspoon of ginger
ice cream of your choice
summer fruits
fresh mint to decorate

Method
In a saucepan, melt the butter, sugar and golden syrup, and mix
until smooth.

In a bowl, sieve the flour and add the ginger. Add the treacle mixture
from the saucepan and work well into the flour.

On a greased tray, place dollops of the mixture and bake in the oven
at 190°C/Gas Mark 5 for 8–10 minutes.

To create each basket shape, mould the brandy circle over an
upside-down bowl, then leave to cool and harden.

To serve – fill the baskets with ice cream and decorate with fresh fruit,
mint and a coulis.

limoncello and yoghurt trifle

Serves 6–8
450g/1 lb of fresh raspberries
3 pots of lemon yoghurt
1 tablespoon of raspberry jam
1 box of sponge fingers – halved
sherry (Amontillado)
Limoncello liqueur

To decorate
double cream
mint sprigs
raspberries

Method
Liquidise the fresh raspberries and the jam to make a coulis.

In a large trifle dish, build layers of sponge, spread with the coulis and a good splash of sherry, add another layer of sponge and a splash of Limoncello liqueur.

Spread plenty of yoghurt over the layers and top with fresh raspberries. Continue to layer the dish until full.

Decorate the top layer with whipped cream, fresh raspberries and mint sprigs.

Leave to cool before serving.

date and chocolate flapjacks

Makes 25 flapjacks

350g/12 oz of dates

150g/5 oz of brown sugar

150g/5 oz of margarine

175g/6 oz of cornflakes

200g/7 oz of chocolate – melted

Method

Melt the margarine in a saucepan and mix with the dates and sugar until a pulp is formed.

Add the cornflakes to the mixture.

Melt the chocolate, then spread the hot mixture in a deep baking tin and pour the chocolate evenly over the top.

Cut into 25 fingers before cooling.

granola

Serves 8

6 cups of quick-cook oats

1 cup of dessicated coconut

½ cup of wheat germ

½ cup of almonds and mixed nuts, broken into small pieces

½ cup of sunflower seeds

½ cup of raisins

⅓ cup of sesame seeds

⅓-⅔ cup of honey

⅓ cup of sunflower oil

⅓ cup of apple or orange juice

Method

In a large bowl, mix all the ingredients together, apart from the raisins.

Cook in a microwave oven at full power for 13–15 minutes, stirring from time to time.

Add the raisins at the last minute of cooking and mix well.

Leave to cool before storing in an airtight container.

To serve – serve with fresh fruit, fruit compôte or yoghurt.

sticky toffee pudding

175g/6 oz of dates
175g/6 oz of caster sugar
175g/6 oz of self-raising flour
50g/2 oz of unsalted butter
275ml/½ pint of water
2 eggs – beaten
2 drops of vanilla essence
1 teaspoon of bicarbonate of soda

The sauce
300ml/½ pint of double cream
50g/2 oz of Demerara sugar
2 teaspoons of black treacle

Method
Prepare a 450g/2 lb loaf tin lined with cling film.

Boil the dates in the water for 2 minutes. Add the bicarbonate of soda.

In a food processor, cream the eggs, sugar and butter before adding the flour
and the vanilla essence. Pour the mixture into the loaf tin and bake on
180°C/Gas Mark 4 for 35–40 minutes.

The sauce – in a saucepan, boil the cream, sugar and treacle until the sugar
has melted to form a smooth sauce.

To serve – serve the pudding warm with a spoonful of sauce.

apple and meringue pudding

Serves 6

8 eating apples – peeled, deseeded and halved

50g/2 oz of butter

50g/2 oz of brown sugar

100ml/3 fl oz of apple juice

juice of 2 limes

zest of 1 lime

½ packet of Digestive biscuits – crushed into crumbs

¼ teaspoon of cinnamon powder

The meringue

6 tablespoons of caster sugar

3 egg whites

1 teaspoon of lemon juice

Method

Heat a frying pan and melt the butter.

Cook the apples for 5–10 minutes until they start to brown.

Pour the sugar into the frying pan and melt – then add the apple juice, the lime zest and juice and the cinnamon and leave to simmer for around 3–4 minutes.

The meringue – in a food mixer, beat the egg whites, add the lemon juice and mix until it is thick enough to be able to stand in peaks.

Add the sugar in three steps, mixing well after each step. The egg white will now be thick.

Transfer the apple mixture to the bottom of an appropriately-sized baking dish. Sprinkle the biscuit crumbs on top of the apple mixture followed by the meringue mixture.

Bake on a high heat (220°C/Gas Mark 7) until the top is crisp and brown.

summer fruits terrine

Serves 8–10

The jelly
7 gelatine leaves
500ml/18 fl oz of fresh orange juice
120g/4½ oz of caster sugar
2 tablespoons of Cointreau (optional)
bunch of fresh mint – finely chopped

The fruit
650g (1½ lbs) mixed fruit of your choice: strawberries, raspberries,
blackberries, cherries etc

Method
The jelly – soften the gelatine leaves in cold water.

Bring the orange juice and caster sugar to the boil in a pan, skim, then
remove from the heat. Add the softened gelatine leaves, and the Cointreau
(if you are using it). Stir for 30 seconds and strain.

Put a thin layer of jelly – ¼" thick – into the terrine, covering the bottom,
add mint leaves along the base and allow to set in the fridge for
approximately 20 minutes.

Place the remaining jelly over ice to cool it down – do not allow to set.

The terrine – when the initial layer of jelly has set, mix all the fruits together
without bruising them, and place in the terrine so that they come to the top.
Press down lightly so that there is as little space as possible between them.

Pour the remaining jelly over the fruits, and add a little chopped mint. Cover
the terrine with cling film, and refrigerate overnight (a minimum of 12 hours).

Before serving, dip the terrine into hot water for a few seconds. Run the
blade of a hot knife down the sides of the dish, keeping the blade tight
against the sides. Turn the terrine out on a plate and carve into slices.

To serve – serve with Llanfaes ice cream.

oranges in cointreau

Serves 4
8 large oranges

The sauce
400g/14 oz of caster sugar
180ml/6 fl oz of orange juice
70ml/2½ fl oz of water
50ml/1¾ fl oz of Cointreau
zest of 2 oranges – finely sliced
fresh mint – to serve

Method
Remove the rind from the oranges.

Slice the oranges into four rounds, keeping them together with a cocktail stick. Place them in a suitable dish.

In a saucepan, heat the caster sugar a little at a time. Stir until all the sugar has dissolved and turned a light golden colour.

Remove the pan from the heat, and add the orange juice and water a little at a time.

Continue stirring and return to the heat to ensure that the sugar has dissolved into the sauce before adding the Cointreau.

Add the zest into the sauce and simmer for 5–10 minutes on a low heat.

Remove from the heat and leave to cool.

Pour over oranges and leave to marinade overnight.

To serve – serve cold decorated with a sprig of mint.

pecan and chocolate brownies

200g/7 oz of plain bitter chocolate (70% cocoa solids) – broken into pieces
165g/5¾ oz of caster sugar
140g/5 oz of plain flour – ifted
120g/4 oz of butter – cubed and softened
100g/3½ oz of pecan nuts – some halved, the rest chopped
2 eggs – beaten
1 teaspoon of vanilla extract
icing sugar – for decorating

Method

Melt the butter and three-quarters of the chocolate in a heat-resistant
glass bowl over a saucepan of simmering water and stir well.

Add the sugar, eggs and vanilla essence and whisk using an electric
beater until evenly blended.

Add the flour and use a spatula to gently fold it through the mixture until
it is a thick, rich, dark batter with no floury areas. Do not overmix.

Prepare a 20cm/8" square baking pan by lining the bottom with
parchment paper.

Smooth the batter out into the tin.

Scatter the nuts and remaining chocolate over the cake, pushing some
well in.

Bake in a preheated oven at 180°C/Gas Mark 4 for 17–18 minutes.

The edges should look firm but the centre barely cooked. The residual
heat will continue the cooking process out of the oven.

Allow to cool a little and then score into 16 squares, sprinkled with
sieved icing sugar.

bitter chocolate tarts

Serves 6
The filling

120g/4½ oz of good quality chocolate (70% cocoa solids) – broken into pieces

100g/3½ oz of kumquats – cut into fine slices

100g/3½ oz of caster sugar

75g/2½ oz of unsalted butter – cut into cubes

50g/1¾ oz of thyme honey

35g/1¼ oz of flour

2 eggs

3 tablespoons of full cream milk

5 tablespoons of crème fraîche

6 sweet crispy pastry tarts 10cm/4" in diameter

0.2 litre/7 fl oz of water

The Sweet Crispy Pastry Tarts

250g/9 oz plain flour

2 egg yolks

2 tablespoons whipping cream

85g/3½ oz icing sugar

pinch of salt

175g/6 oz unsalted butter, cubed

Method

In a saucepan over a low heat, place the kumquat slices, granulated sugar and water. Bring to the boil and allow to crystallise gently on a low, simmering heat for about 1 hour.

Melt the chocolate slowly in a bowl set over a panful of hot (not boiling) water.

Pour the milk, crème fraîche and butter into a saucepan. Bring to the boil, remove from the heat and allow to cool.

In a bowl, beat the eggs, add the thyme honey, and beat again. Gradually incorporate the flour into the egg mixture and whisk until blended.

Add the melted chocolate and whisk.

bitter chocolate tarts

Add the milk, crème fraîche and butter.

Whisk well and allow to rest for about 1 hour in the fridge.

The Sweet Crispy Pastry Tarts – Sift the flour into a large bowl. Rub the butter into the flour until the consistency is like breadcrumbs.

Beat the egg yolks, the cream, the sugar and the salt together in a bowl, then add to the flour and butter.

Mix to form a light dough. Knead lightly before wrapping the dough in clingfilm and chilling in the fridge for an hour. This is a crumbly pastry, so handle it with care. It will need to be taken out of the fridge 15 minutes before using.

Roll the pastry to a thickness of 3mm and line six 4cm non-stick tart tins (any other kind of tins will need greasing). Trim away any surplus pastry, and chill in the fridge for half an hour before using.

Bake for 10 minutes before filling.

To finish – divide the chocolate mixture between the tarts, smooth the surface and cook in the oven at 180°C/Gas Mark 4 for 6 to 7 minutes (according to the oven).

Meanwhile, arrange the crystallised kumquat slices around the edge of each plate and add a little of the cooking syrup.

When the chocolate tarts are cooked, take them out of the oven, and place one in the middle of each plate. Serve immediately.

N.B. When cooked, the centre of each tart should be runny.

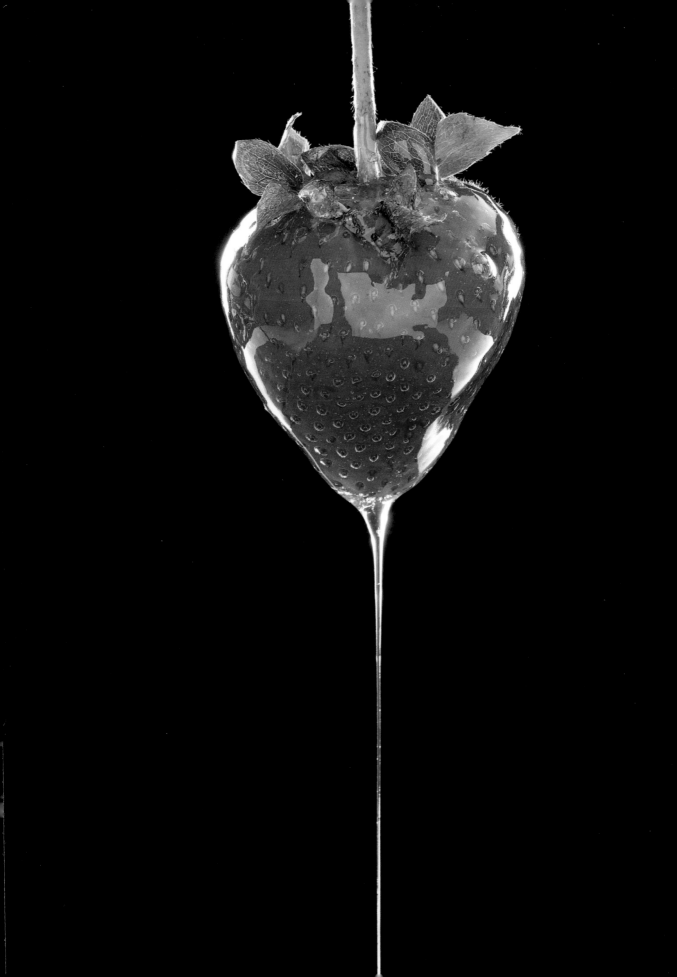

For a full list of books currently in print, send now for your free copy of our new, full-colour catalogue – or simply surf into our website at **www.ylolfa.com.**

Y Lolfa Cyf., Talybont, Ceredigion SY24 5AP
e-mail ylolfa@ylolfa.com
www.ylolfa.com
tel +44 (0)1970 832 304
fax 832 782
isdn 832 813